eDiscovery Nuts and Bolts:

The Essentials of E-Discovery For Identity Theft Prevention and Protection

EDRM

Electronic Discovery Reference Model

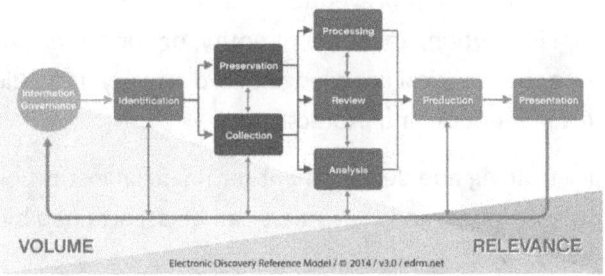

By

Anthony Johnson

DISCLAIMER

Nothing contained in this ebook textbook should be construed as being legal advice. The legal information herein is based upon knowledge, skill, experience, and training developed over 20 years of working in the legal field as a consumer advocate, litigation support, mediator, arbitrator, negotiator, E-Discovery Consultant and House Counsel, as well as a victim of identity theft and perpetrator thereof for purposes of writing this ebook.

This ebook is designed to illuminate the "nuts and bolts" of e-discovery for identity theft prevention and protection. Whether you are a financial institution, government entity, or consumer, this guide will punctuate the practical knowledge of e-discovery as applied to identity theft prevention and protection.

Further training and development for financial institutions, business, organizations, and consumers can be ascertained by tuning into internet radio at

www.blogtalkradio.com/e-discoverynutsandbolts

or visit our website at:

www.ediscoverynow.net

for our training schedule.

Introduction

In the computer age, 99% of all documents are created and stored electronically. With the press of a computer key, an e-mail can be sent around the world. Today, all litigants, pro se or otherwise, have a duty to request and disclose responsive electronic evidence in their cases. Whether your case is large or small, identity theft prevention or protection, discovery issues relating to electronic evidence will have to be addressed and resolved.

Electronic evidence has been described as e-mail, spreadsheets, word processing documents, audio, video, or any other content that has metastasized in a digital format. This includes data base electronic evidence from the three major credit reporting agencies, to wit: Trans-Union, Experian, and Equifax. The fact-finding process will require you to uncover electronic evidence, and at some point require you to have a working knowledge of how to request and disclose responsive electronic evidence in efforts to prevent identity theft or protect yourself from the perpetration thereof.

Like it or not, e-discovery is here to stay. The voluminous nature of data creation is making it more difficult to coral relevant electronically stored information ("ESI"). Identity theft is the fastest growing crime in the country, according to the credit bureau TransUnion, with almost 10 million incidents per year. In fact, the bureau calculates that every minute, 19 people become victims, and the average cost to the victim is $500.00 and 30 hours of hassle. It will be your job as investigator to find a way to utilize self-directed workable solutions in efforts to corral ESI from the credit reporting agencies, financial institutions, and government entities, and:

- Define scope parameters
- Determine relevancy
- Create timelines for production or e-depositions

- Propose confidential compromises
- Create efficiencies with a mutual discovery plan
- Create boundaries for preservation
- Avoid spoliation pitfalls
- Manage protection of privileged information
- Maintain credibility with the court
- Avoid court-imposed sanctions, and
- Allocate costs

Remember, effective December 1, 2006, the revised Federal Rules of Civil Procedure 26 and 34 allow for the discovery of electronically stored information that is "reasonably accessible."

IDENTITY THEFT PROTECTION

Your credit report, which is available by contacting the three main repositories (TransUnion, Experian, and Equifax) will be your starting point.   Once you have your credit report, you can enlist the support of your bank or financial institution to head off the identity theft before it metastasizes.

There are some basic steps you my take to prevent identity theft:

1. If you lose your wallet, purse, or credit card, contact your card issuer right away.
2. Avoid using ATM's in obscure locations because it's easier for thieves to install "skimming" devices on them that steal your information when you swipe your card.
3. Check your account statements for errors.
4. Look for mistakes on your credit report. (It would be a good idea to consult a credit monitoring service that will alert you via email when a new account is opened).
5. Respond to calls or letters from your bank. (Failure to respond to calls or letters could allow the perpetration of identity theft).

6. Follow up on odd bills you receive. (This is the number signal that your identity may have been compromised).
7. Stay on top of missing mail. (If you don't receive bank statements as usual, this could signal a problem).
8. Follow up if you receive unexpected mail. (This too could signal that a "COA" Change of Address has been initiated with the post office and your mailing address has been altered).
9. Look out for errors on your Social Security Statement of account.
10. Investigate if you're denied an application based on your credit.

The above 10 steps are just the tip of the iceberg, the basics to look out for with identity thieves. However, identity thieves are getting smarter, more sophisticated, and staying ahead of the game. Authorities say there is a new twist on identity theft: **Synthetic Identity Fraud.**

Synthetic Identity Fraud is when the fraudster uses one true piece of your identity, and then, combines it with fake information, i.e., a different date of birth, social security number, address, etc.

Synthetic Identity Fraud now accounts for approximately 85% of all identity fraud in the United States, costing an estimated $2 billion per year, according to investigators. Synthetic Identity Fraud can be perpetrated by the use of "CPN's" or Credit Profile Numbers, by credit repair companies. But CPN's are just a fraction of how this fraud can metastasize. The other way Synthetic Identity Fraud can be initiated is by using a similar name, with a different address, which can be created on a credit profile by default with the application of credit.

To combat this new type of fraud, one must be vigilant. One way stifle the fraud is to place a "Credit Bureau Message" on your credit report. This can be accomplished by simply writing to the three major credit bureaus with a statement, to wit:

"Please DO NOT issue any credit under my name without first contacting me at this phone number 999-999-9999 to verify that I have in fact applied for credit. "

This simple Credit Bureau Message or "Fraud Alert" will prevent any attempts for anyone to commit identity theft, synthetic identity theft, or any other type of theft or fraud in your name because the credit issuing agency will have to contact you first and inquire if you have in fact applied for credit! This has been the best way to prevent identity theft for me.   Since I have employed this method years ago, creditors always call me when I apply for credit, lines of credit, car loans, etc., to verify that I have in fact applied for credit.

If you have already been the victim of identity theft, then, you must dig a little deeper and employ this strategy: File an **I.D. Theft Affidavit or FTC Fraud Affidavit.** This affidavit will illuminate the trade lines that have been opened in your name under fraud. You must attach a police report with the affidavit and submit it to the three (3) major credit bureaus. Once that is done, request that a "credit freeze" be placed in your credit file as well as a credit bureau message. The credit freeze and bureau message will act as a "stop-gap" measure to prevent creditors from extending credit in your name without first contacting you to verify that you have in fact applied for credit.

Identity Theft Prevention

Banks and financial institutions have come a long way to combat identity theft and fraud. Some are better than others. There are many ways to perpetrate identity theft and obtain money, goods, and services using someone else's good name. We've all read about the data breaches at department stores, banks, and government agencies. That is the sophisticated "high tech" method. There are still very lucrative "low tech" ways that identity theft can metastasize and financial institutions need to employ some basic steps to prevent "low tech" identity theft from transpiring on their watch.

Here are a few simple steps that can be added to a financial institutions fraud department to stop identity theft:

1. Watch for a new address to extend credit that is not reflected on the credit report. People move, however, it would be prudent to send a letter to the old address stating that credit has been requested with a new address, and to have the person call to confirm that credit has in fact been requested.
2. When credit is requested, and there is a new address that is not reflected on the credit report, cross check the identifying information with one of the other credit accounts on the credit report and call the financial institution. Explain that you are calling from the fraud department of your bank, and you need to obtain a current address and phone number for the person seeking to obtain credit at your bank.
3. If the financial institution is a nationwide institution, have the person applying for credit come in and bring a government issued photo identification, along with another credit card, and utility bill for the new address, before extending credit.
4. Verify the work phone, email, and URL of the employer. Call the employer and ask for the perpetrator by name. Have the employer transfer the call to the extension of the person seeking credit.
5. Cross check the work phone number with directory assistance. Double check the presumptive employee with Human Resources.

This may seem time consuming, but if financial institutions are serious about stopping identity theft, especially low tech, forensic identity theft and fraud, these steps are very easy to follow and could save your institution millions of dollars in lost revenue from fraudulent purchases and cash withdrawals.

If the identity theft is beyond the point of return, and litigation has become imminent, pending or impending, you will need to know how to request and disclosure responsive electronic data from the credit bureaus and creditors themselves.

The Electronic Discovery Reference Model (EDRM) will be your guide and as a consumer and you will need to become familiar with each stage of the model.

During the **Identification, Preservation & Collection** stage, the consumer will need to take the riskiest steps first: making quick, defensible decisions about what data you will need, then preserving that ESI. Why risky? Because if you get it wrong you may never get a second chance to do it right.

During the **Processing** stage, the consumer will need to process the data. You will need to become adept at offering suggestions on how to control processing scope, timeframe, and costs as well as pull the cover off so you can see what actually happens during processing.

During the **Analysis** stage, the consumer will need to become accustomed to key word searching. Key word searching is the bread and butter of e-discovery analysis, built on approaches developed during more than three decades of automated litigation support. Then, there is the "New Analysis" or "CAR/TAR/Predictive Coding". This new wave of analytical tools are upon us, going by many names—the most customary being predictive coding, technology assisted review (TAR), and computer assisted review (CAR).

The **Review and Production** stage is often the largest cost. The consumer can look like a genius by managing review for relevance and privileged information efficiently and effectively while still delivering acceptable, defensible results.

Budgeting. We all know that nothing in life is free—especially not e-discovery. The consumer who knows how to effectively budget the e-discovery project will harness the skills to be able to predict costs at the onset of the matter, track costs to avoid overruns, and project likely future costs.

New Rules relating to e-discovery. Every consumer should familiarize themselves with their states new rules that relates to the preservation, discoverability, production, accessibility, and costs associated with ESI, which includes e-mail, word processing documents, spreadsheets, voice mail, databases, and more. Most state's rules are modeled after the Federal Rules which took effect on December 1, 2006.

Has that gotten your attention?

Do you have some idea of how the role of a consumer for e-discovery may just be the tool that has been missing from the toolbox that is necessary in efforts to fix identity theft?

Do you understand that ascertaining documentary evidence, whether in paper or electronic form, will be synonymous with ascertaining compelling evidence as a consumer in your efforts to reverse identity theft that may have been perpetrated against you?

Are you beginning to believe that the consumers who have taken time to understand electronic discovery will have a powerful position to stop and reverse the fraud in relation to those who may be ignorant about e-discovery?

If so, continue to read on...

TABLE OF CONTENTS

PROLOGUE

The Electronic Discovery Reference Model (EDRM)

EDRM

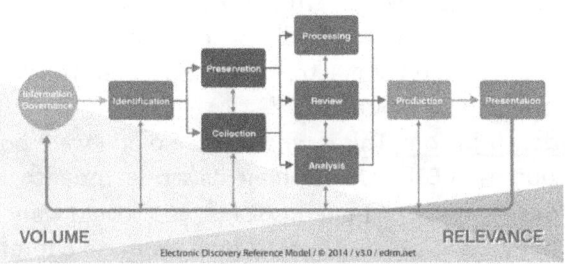

The Electronic Discovery Reference Model (EDRM) was initially conceived by George Socha, Jr., founder of Socha Consulting, LLC in St. Paul, MN, and Tom Gelbmann, managing director of Gelbmann & Associates, in Roseville, MN. The reference model divides the e-discovery process into six areas:

- Information Management
- Identification
- Preservation|Collection
- Processing|Review|Analysis
- Production
- Presentation

The EDRM identifies the functions associated with each area. It has been said that if you don't have experience in e-discovery, the

11

EDRM is useful because it is good for showing what the issues are. The EDRM is also useful as a guide to move you along the process of identifying data and subsequently preserving that data, collecting it, processing it, and so on.

Let's take a moment to familiarize ourselves with a summary of explanations of each EDRM stage.

- **Information Management**: This is where a company should begin to get their electronic house in order to mitigate risk and expenses should e-discovery become an issue, from initial creation of electronically stored information through its final disposition.
- **Identification**: This is where you would locate potential sources of ESI and determine its scope, breadth, and depth.
- **Preservation**: During this stage, you would want to ensure that ESI is protected against inappropriate alteration or destruction.
- **Collection**: Collection is the gathering of ESI for further use in the discovery process, i.e., processing, review, etc.
- **Processing**: This is where you would reduce the volume of ESI and convert it, if necessary, to forms more suitable for review and analysis.
- **Review**: To evaluate ESI for relevance and privilege.
- **Analysis**: This is where you would evaluate ESI for content & context, including key patterns, topics, people and discussion.
- **Production**: To deliver ESI to others in appropriate forms and using appropriate delivery mechanisms.
- **Presentation**: Displaying ESI before audiences (at depositions, hearings, trials, etc.), especially in native and

near-native forms, to elicit further information, validate existing facts or positions, or persuade an audience.

Now that we have that covered, let's take a look at the basics of E-Discovery and tie it all in...

CHAPTER I
The Basics of Electronic Discovery

Electronic discovery has been described as the "disclosure or discovery of electronically stored information (ESI), including the form or forms in which it should be produced..." See, Junk v. Aon Corp., No. 07-4640, 2007 U.S. Dist. LEXIS 89741, at *2 n.2 (D.N.Y. Nov. 30, 2007). ESI includes e-mail, spreadsheets, word processing documents, audio, video, instant or text messaging, personal information systems, and databases. Electronic discovery is considered to be the request, collection, review, production, and management of electronic information.

Metadata

Unlike traditional paper discovery, electronic data files will include "metadata," or what is known as additional hidden data. Metadata is defined as data providing more information about one or more aspects of the existing data. Metadata may include:

- **Means of creation of the data**
- **Purpose of the data**
- **Time and date of creation**
- **Creation or author of data**
- **Location on a computer network where the data was created**
- **Standards used to create the data**

This valuable information does not appear on the printed copy of an electronic file. Metadata is found in e-mail messages, word processing documents, spreadsheets, audio, video, and other digital files. E-mail metadata may contain who was blind copied on a message. A computer will contain information about Internet usage

14

such as which websites were visited, when, and by whom. Metadata is an important aspect of ESI because it may very well be more valuable than the traditional forms of evidence in building or defending a case.

Think about metadata in this concept: If you believe that your determination was based upon discrimination, you have a duty to request, and your employer would have a duty to disclose, any information relating to your job performance, performance reviews, raises, records of attendance, absenteeism, etc. Most of these documents would be kept in electronic format. The metadata would be that hidden data that would illuminate the time and date of the entry of the data, who had entered the data, what entity had entered the data, the location on the database network where the data was created, etc. During mediation, you should request information to be produced in native file format so that you may capture that all-important metadata.

Spoliation

Don't be overly concerned about the destruction of or manipulation of ESI. The failure to produce ESI can lead to very severe consequences for the culprit. These consequences may include:

- **Malpractice**
- **Imposition of court sanctions**
- **Loss of an otherwise winnable case**
- **Summary judgment in your favor**
- **Disciplinary action**

In efforts to punctuate the severity of spoliation of evidence, there are two landmark decisions I'd like you to review:

1. <u>Coleman (Parent) Holdings, Inc. v. Morgan Stanley & Co., Inc.</u>, 2005 WL 67071 (Fla. Cir. Ct. Mar. 1, 2005), rev'd on other grounds, 955 So.2d 1124 (Fla. 4th CA 2007), and
2. <u>Zubulake v. UBS Warburg, LLC</u>, 229 F.R.D. 422 (D.N.Y. 2004).

In these decisions, the court issued adverse inference instructions for spoliation of evidence. As a result, the jury in the <u>Morgan Stanley</u> case returned with a $1.4 billion verdict; and the jury in <u>Zubulake</u> returned with a $29 million verdict.

*Note: Spoliation of evidence is the intentional or negligent withholding, hiding, altering, or destroying of evidence relevant to a legal proceeding. See, *Wikipedia.org*.

Federal and State Rules Relating to ESI

On December 1, 2006, changes relating to electronically stored information (ESI) in the Federal Rules of Civil Procedure metastasized. The changes affected Rules 16, 26, 33, 34, 37, 45 and Form 35 and provided mandates to the preservation, discoverability, production, accessibility, and costs associated with ESI. Federal courts have issued local rules of practice and guidelines regarding ESI. Visit www.elawexchange.com under the section entitled "Leading Decisions and Fed. Rules" for a more comprehensive look at the framework for the discovery of electronic data.

For an up-to-date listing of state-by-state electronic discovery case decisions and procedural rules, visit www.elawexchange.com for online access. And, don't forget to check your state's court rules in relation to electronic discovery and evidence!

CHAPTER 2
Forms, Types, and Storage of ESI

There are many different forms of electronically stored information (ESI) that should be considered in your quest to uncover relevant evidence. Principal "forms" that should be considered when discussing the disclosure of ESI should include:

- **Native File**
- **Database**
- **Spreadsheet**
- **Image**
- **ASCII, TEXT, and Conversion Formats, i.e., .PDF and .TIFF**
- **Video and Audio**
- **Paper**
- **ALS and Online ESI Repository**

Also, there are different "types" of ESI, as well, including:

- **E-mail**
- **Word Processing Documents**
- **Spreadsheets**
- **Voicemail messages and files**
- **Backup email files**
- **Deleted Emails**
- **Data files**
- **Program files**
- **Backup Archival Tapes**
- **Temporary files**
- **System History Files**

*Note: Request the forms of ESI that are most advantageous to your needs, i.e., native file format to view hidden metadata.

Another important topic of consideration should concern the possible storage media, devices, and locations of ESI. Understanding these areas will not only help you pinpoint the discovery of relevant ESI, but also the production of ESI.

Storage Media

Storage media is used to store data from an electronic device. These storage devices could include a floppy disc, hard drive, thumb drive, CD-ROM, DVD, Blu-ray Disk, Smart Card, and Microfilm/Microfiche.

Storage Devices

Storage devices use the storage media discussed above. The storage devices are the places where the storage media must be placed in efforts to see, hear and enjoy the data. Some of the most common storage devices include a mainframe computer, printer, copier, personal computer, laptop, PDA, cell phone, voice mail, pager, and scanner.

Just think of the storage device as the place where that DVD or thumb drive needs to be placed in order to view the data once you receive it from the producing party.

Storage Locations

The location is the place where the actual "physical" data can be found. This is one of the most important challenges of uncovering relevant electronic data, which is why you will need to conduct an Electronic Discovery Identification and Preservation Questionnaire, which is designed to help identify, preserve and collect electronically stored information for discovery. Storage locations may include Service

Providers for the Internet, Satellite, Pagers, Cellular phones, Financial Institutions/Credit Card Issuers, Credit Bureau Repositories, Cable Service Providers, as well as Internet Storage Locations such as the World Wide Web, chat rooms, newsgroups, Facebook, LinkedIn, Cache files, etc.

The purpose of the Electronic Discovery Identification and Preservation Questionnaire is for you to gain an understanding of the producing party's computer system so that you have a working knowledge of how their ESI is created, stored, and retained. Remember the words "native file format" mentioned at the top of the chapter? Well, that simply means the way that a data file is "reasonably usable" or "ordinarily maintained". That would mean that the data format is proprietary and not transferrable unless a conversion software is used.

Example: Microsoft Excel is saved in proprietary format with the file extension .XLS. In Excel, you can open, modify, and save any changes to the file. If you wanted to use the same file in Lotus 1-2-3, then, a conversion process would need to be performed on the .XLS file. The conversion process may not accurately convert the file in the new Lotus format because metadata may be lost inadvertently.

Note: Courts have held that a producing party should provide electronic discovery in its native file format. The scrubbing or erasing metadata from native files without agreement of the requesting party is sanctionable conduct. Producing ESI in native file format allows a party to view the original document including any metadata and tracked changes. The failure to ask for "metadata" in the original request may preclude later discovery of the all-important hidden data. And, courts have consistently held that disclosure in a .TIFF or .PDF format, as opposed to a "native file" format is unusable, notwithstanding a party's ability to redact and Bates-stamp .TIFF images.

CHAPTER 3
<u>Some Important Rules You Can Use</u>

As previously mentioned, on December 1, 2006, changes relating to the preservation, discoverability, production, accessibility, and costs associated with electronically stored information (ESI) took effect in the Federal Rules of Civil Procedure. These changes will impact most cases in federal court and your state court may have changes that will mirror the federal changes.

We will not attempt to peruse every nook and cranny of the rules, state or federal, but will highlight some important decisions relating to the discoverability of ESI to give you a working knowledge of their importance, and allow you the opportunity to speak intelligently at your upcoming Rule 26(f) "Meet and Confer" conference or your state level Case Management Conference in regards to the request and production of electronically stored information.

Rules Requiring Cooperation Between Parties

Federal Rules of Civil Procedure 16(a): The court may order a pretrial conference of all parties for such purposes as:
- **Expediting disposition**
- **Establishing early and continuing control of a case**
- **Discourage wasteful pretrial activities**
- **Improve the quality through more thorough preparation**
- **Facilitation of settlement**

Federal Rules of Civil Procedure 26(a)(1): Parties must, without awaiting discovery request, disclose to other parties:
- **Witnesses who may have discoverable information and description and location of ESI relevant to the case**

- **Computation of each category of damages claimed and make evidentiary material available for inspection and copying, unless privileged or protected from disclosure**

Federal Rules of Civil Procedure 26(b)(2)(C): Provides the Courts the inherent authority to limit discovery *sua sponte* or on motion if:

- **Requests are unreasonably cumulative or duplicative**
- **Requests are obtainable from more convenient, less burdensome or inexpensive source**
- **A party has had plenty of opportunity to obtain information during action, and burden or expense of proposed discovery outweighs likely benefit in light of case needs, amount in controversy, parties' resources, importance of issues and of discovery to those issues**

Federal Rules of Civil Procedure 26(f): Conference Planning Obligations aka "Meet and Confer". The parties must meet as soon as practicable to:

- **Consider possibilities for settlement/resolution**
- **Arrange disclosures required by Rule 26(a)(1)**
- **Discuss issues about preserving ESI**
- **Disclose custodian name and discoverable data sources**
- **Develop a discovery plan and written report**

Federal Rules of Civil Procedure 26(g): Certification. Every disclosure and discovery request, response, or objection must be signed by at least one attorney of record certifying the disclosure is complete and correct to best of their knowledge, information and belief formed after:

- **Reasonable inquiry that the disclosures were complete and correct at the time made**

- **Discovery requests and responses are consistent with existing law**
- **Not interposed for improper purpose**
- **Neither unreasonable nor unduly burdensome or expensive in light of case needs, amount in controversy, and importance of issues at stake**

Important ESI Case Law and Legal Hold

In order to truly understand the importance and relevance of ESI case law, you must first understand the concept of the "**litigation hold**" or "**legal hold**". Remember, the litigation hold, or legal hold is one of the most important, if not **the** most important part of the entire litigation. This directive is an ongoing process to preserve electronically stored information, documents, or physical evidence pertaining to "reasonably anticipated" litigation. If you are a pro se litigant, you would not issue a legal hold per se, but would issue a "**Data Preservation Notice or Request**" to opposing counsel about what has been preserved, what you would like preserved, and request his or her reasonable input as to whether other ESI needs to be preserved.

1. Zubulake v. UBS Warbug, LLC, 220 F.R.D. 212, 218 (S.D.N.Y. 2003) (Scheindlin, S.)("[o]nce a party reasonably anticipates litigation, it must suspend its routine document retention/destruction policy and put in place a legal hold to ensure the preservation of relevant documents").

2. Pension Comm. Of the Univ. of Montreal Pension Plan v. Banc of Am. Secs, LLC, No. 05-9016, 2010 U.S. Dist. LEXIS 4546 (S.D.N.Y. Jan. 15, 2010), as corrected, Docket #358 (May 28, 2010)("[a] plaintiff's duty is more often triggered before litigation commences, in large part because plaintiffs control the timing of litigation").

3. <u>Victor Stanley, Inc. v. Creative Pipe, Inc. "Victor Stanley II"</u>, U.S. Dist. LEXIS 93644 (D. Md. Sept. 9, 2010), where U.S. District Judge Paul W. Grimm provided counsel with "an analytical framework that may enable them to resolve preservation/spoliation issues with a greater level of comfort that their actions will not expose them to disproportionate costs or unpredictable outcomes of spoliation motions." The court's discussion also included numerous key points and a "Law of Spoliation" framework that outlines the scope of duty to preserve among other culpability and prejudice requirements in each of the federal circuits.

Depending on the common law of your jurisdiction, the duty to preserve relevant evidence arises when litigation is "reasonably anticipated"; "pending, imminent, reasonably foreseeable"; "pending or impending". Again, consult Judge Grimm's "Law of Spoliation" framework for guidance on what the common law of your jurisdiction may be with respect to preservation of evidence.

One final caveat: **A document retention policy that repeatedly and automatically destroys electronically stored information on a consistent and timely schedule without any regards to any legal hold directive will face severe consequences if the policy is not modified to suspend the destruction once litigation is reasonably anticipated.**

Sample Legal Hold

LITIGATION HOLD NOTICE

Dear Litigation and IT Personnel,

Please be advised that this communication constitutes a formal request to preserve any and all relevant data in efforts to facilitate the collection of data in relation to (your type of case) in regards to the circumstances surrounding (your name here). I believe electronically stored information ("ESI" hereinafter) to be an important and irreplaceable source of discovery and/or evidence in this matter. The facilitation of a resolution will require preservation of all information from your companies' computer systems, removable electronic media, and other locations. This includes, but is not limited to, email and other electronic communication, word processing documents, spreadsheets, databases, calendars, telephone logs, contact manager information, Internet usage files, and network access information.

Your company should also preserve the following platforms in the possession of Your Company or a third party under the control of Your Company (such as an employee or outside vendor under contract): databases, networks, computer systems, including legacy systems (hardware and software), servers, archives, backup or disaster recovery systems, tapes, discs, drives, cartridges and other storage media, laptops, personal computers, internet data, personal digital assistants, handheld wireless devices, mobile telephones, paging devices, and audio systems (including voicemail).

All of the information contained in the letter should be preserved for the following dates and time periods: (Enter relevant time period)

Preservation Obligations

The laws and rules prohibiting destruction of evidence apply to electronically stored information in the same manner that they apply to other evidence. See, e.g., In re Amendments to the (Your State Rules of Civil Procedure—Electronic Discovery; see also, Federal Rules of Civil Procedure, effective December 1, 2006. Due to its format, electronic information is easily deleted, modified or corrupted. Accordingly, (Your Company) must take every reasonable step to preserve this information until the final resolution of this matter. *See, e.g., Coleman (Parent) Holdings, Inc. v. Morgan Stanley & Co., Inc.,* 2005 WL 67071 (Fla. Cir. Ct. Mar. 1, 2005), *rev'd on other grounds*, 955 So.2d 1124 (Fla. 4th Cir. CA 2007); and *Zubulake v. UBS Warburg*, LLC, 229 F.R.D. 422 (D.N.Y. 2004), (where the Courts issued adverse inference instructions for spoliation of evidence. As a result, the jury in the Morgan Stanley case returned with a $1.4 billion verdict and in Zubulake the jury returned with a $29 million verdict).

This includes an obligation to:

- Discontinue all data destruction and backup tape recycling policies;
- Preserve and not dispose of relevant hardware unless an exact replica of the file (a mirror image) is made;
- Preserve and not destroy passwords, decryption procedures (and accompany software), network access codes, ID names, manuals, tutorials, written instructions, decompression or reconstruction software;
- Maintain all other pertinent information and tools needed to access, review, and reconstruct necessary to access, view and/or reconstruct all requested or potentially relevant electronic data.

Description of Data Sought

The facilitation of this workplace confliction resolution and potential lawsuit requires the preservation of all information from Your Company's computer systems, removable electronic media and other locations relating to the circumstances surrounding the termination of (Your Name Here). This includes, but is not limited to, email and other electronic communication, word processing documents, spreadsheets, databases, calendars, telephone logs, contact manager information, Internet usage files, and network access information.

I. **Electronic Files**. You have an obligation to preserve all digital or analog electronic files in electronic format, regardless of whether hard copies of the information exist. This includes preserving:
   a. Active data (i.e., data immediately and easily accessible on Your Company's systems today);
   b. Archived data (i.e., data residing on backup tapes or other storage media);
   c. Deleted data (i.e., data that has been deleted from a computer hard drive but is recoverable through computer forensic techniques); and
   d. Legacy data (i.e., data created on old or obsolete hardware or software);
   e. Your Company must preserve active, archived and legacy data including but not limited to:
      i. Word-processing files, including drafts and revisions;
      ii. Spreadsheets, including drafts and revisions;
      iii. Databases;
      iv. CAD (computer-aided design) files, including drafts and revisions;
      v. Presentation data or slide shows produced by presentation software (such as Microsoft PowerPoint);
      vi. Graphs, charts or other data produced by project management software (such as Microsoft Project);
      vii. Animations, images, audio, video and audiovisual recordings, MP3 players, and voicemail files;
      viii. Data generated by calendaring, task management and personal information management (PIM) software (such as Microsoft Outlook or Lotus Notes);
      ix. Data created with the use of personal data assistants (PDA's), such as PalmPilot, HP Jornada; Cassiopeia or other Windows CE-based or Pocket PC

           devices;

      x. Data created with the use of document management software; and

      xi. Data created with the use of paper and electronic mail logging and routing software.

    f. Your Company must preserve media used by its computers including but not limited to:

        i. Magnetic, optical or other storage media, including the hard drives or floppy disks used by its computers;

        ii. Backup media (i.e., other hard drives, backup tapes, floppies, Jaz cartridges, CD-ROMs), and the software necessary to reconstruct the data contained on the media; and

        iii. Archived media (you should retain a mirror image or copy of any media no longer in service but used during the following time periods);

           1. (Relevant time period)

II.   **Hardware.** Your Company has an obligation to preserve all electronic processing systems, even if they are replaced. This includes computer servers, stand-alone personal computers, hard drives, laptops, PDA's, and other electronic processing devices. Your Company should retain copies of any hardware no longer in service but used during the time periods:

           1. (Relevant time period)

III.   **Emails.** Your Company has an obligation to preserve all potentially relevant internal and external emails that were sent or received surrounding the workplace conflict under investigation. Email must be preserved in electronic format, regardless of whether hard copies of the information exist.

IV.   **Internet Web Activity.** Your Company has an obligation to preserve all records of Internet and Web-browser generated files in electronic format, regardless of whether hard copies of the information exist. This includes Internet and Web-browser-generated history files, caches and "cookies" files stored on backup media or generated by an individual employed at Your Company.

V.   **Activity Logs.** Your Company must preserve all hard copy or electronic logs documenting computer use by Your Company.

VI.   **Supporting Information.** Your Company must preserve all supporting information relating to the requested electronic data and/or media including;

    a. Codebooks, keys,, data dictionaries, diagrams, handbooks, or other supporting documents that aid in reading or interpreting database, media, email, hardware, software, or activity log information.

VII. **Information for Employees.** Your Company should preserve all data that contains the information described below for the following employees **WHO ARE CUSTODIANS OF RELEVANT DATA:**

    a. The following information is requested on the above-listed persons:

        i. Basic employee information, including name, date of birth, employee identification number, race, date hired (or rehired), date fired, and educational background;

        ii. Employment performance evaluations or reviews;

        iii. All information, including W-2 forms, relating to compensation (including salary, bonuses, merit increases, stock options or other forms of compensation);

        iv. For each position held by the employee during (relevant time period), list the job title/position, salary level, function or description, location, department, subsidiary, time in position, and job status (covered or not covered), and whether the employee was full-time, part-time or temporary;

      v. Any disciplinary action or employment contract violations; or

     vi. If the individual is a former employee, list the date of departure and reason for leaving.

VIII. **Other Relevant Information**.

    a. Documents relating to computer systems, programs, software, hardware, materials, tools or information that Your Company uses or used to track, monitor or prevent discriminatory employment practices.

    b. From (relevant time period), all documents that relate to any software or hardware computer changes affecting Your Company's database.

Description of Documents And Media That Should Be Preserved

IX. **Data Preservation.** Your Company should immediately preserve all data and information about the data (i.e., backup activity logs and document retention policies) relating to documents maintained in the ordinary course of business for the employees listed in Section VII above. This includes, but is not limited to, the following:

    a. Email and any relevant metadata, including message contents, header information, and email system logs that was sent or received by or is in the possession of the following parties and/or contains information about the circumstances surrounding the **RELEVANT TIME PERIOD;**

    b. All active and deleted copies of any word processing files, spreadsheets, PowerPoint presentations, or other documents that are in the possession of the following parties and/or contain information about the circumstances surrounding the **RELEVANT TIME PERIOD;**

    c. Databases and any information about the databases that are in the possession of the parties responsible for maintaining the information about the circumstances surrounding the **RELEVANT TIME PERIOD;**

    d. All paper and/or electronic logs of computer system and network activity that pertain to electronic data storage that are in the possession of the parties responsible for maintaining the information surrounding the **RELEVANT TIME PERIOD;**

    e. All active and deleted copies of any electronic calendars or scheduling programs, including programs maintained on PDA's, that are in the possession of the parties responsible for maintaining the information surrounding the **RELEVANT TIME PERIOD;**

    f. All active, archived, legacy, and deleted copies of any other electronic data that are in the possession of the parties responsible for maintaining the information surrounding the **RELEVANT TIME PERIOD.**

X. **Data Storage Devices**.

    a. *Online Storage Data.* If Your Company uses online storage and/or direct access storage devices, they must immediately case modifying or deleting any electronic data unless a computer forensic expert makes a mirror image of the electronic file, follows proper preservation protocols for assuring the accuracy of the file (i.e., chain of custody), and makes the file available for litigation.

    b. *Offline Data Storage.* Offline data includes, but is not limited to, backup and archival media, floppy diskettes, magnetic, magneto-optical, and/or optical tapes and cartridges, DVD's, CDROM's, and other removable media. Your Company should immediately suspend all activity that might result in destruction or modification of all of the data stored on any offline media. This includes overwriting, recycling, or erasing all or part of the media. This request includes, but is not limited to, media used to store data from personal computers, laptops, mainframe computers, and servers.

c. *Data Storage Device Replacement.* If Your Company replace(s) any electronic data storage devices, Your Company may not dispose of the storage devices.

d. *Preservation of Storage Devices.* Your Company may not modify, delete or otherwise alter (i.e., by data compression, disk de-fragmentation, or optimization routines) any electronic data unless a computer forensic expert makes a mirror image of the electronic file, follows proper preservation protocols for assuring the accuracy of the file (i.e., chain of custody), and makes the file available in event it is needed for litigation. The expert must make a mirror image of active files, restored versions of deleted files, and restored versions of deleted file fragments, hidden files, and directory listings. This includes, but is not limited to, preserving electronic data (stored on online or offline storage devices) that came from the following hardware or software applications:

    i. Fixed drives on stand-alone personal computers or laptops;
    ii. Network servers and workstations; and
    iii. Software application programs and utilities.

Preservation Compliance

XI. **Activity Log.** In order to show preservation compliance, (Your Company) must maintain a log, documenting all alterations or deletions made to any electronic data storage device or any electronic data processing system. The log should include changes and deletions made by supervisors, employees, contractors, vendors, or any other third parties.

XII. **Mirror Images.** (Your Company) must secure a mirror image copy (bit-by-bit copy of a hard drive that ensures the computer system is not altered during the imaging process) of all electronic data contained on the personal computers and/or laptops of the individuals listed below. The mirror image should include active files, deleted file fragments, hidden files, directories, and any other data contained on the computer. Your Company must also collect and store any offline or online storage devices that contain data from any electronic processing devices for the individuals listed in Paragraph VII above.

XIII. **Chain of Custody.** For each piece of media that (Your Company) preserves, it must document a complete chain of custody. A proper chain of custody will ensure that no material changes, alterations or modifications were made while the evidence was handled. Chain of custody documentation must indicate where the media has been, whose possession it has been in, and the reason for that possession.

XIV. **Electronic Data Created After This Letter.** For any electronic data created after this letter or for any electronic processing systems used after this letter, (Your Company) must take the proper steps to avoid destroying potentially relevant evidence. This includes following all of the above preservation protocols.

Wherefore, compliance with the preservation obligations as illuminated above includes forwarding a copy of this letter to all individuals or organizations that are responsible for any of the items referred to in this letter. If this correspondence is in any respect unclear, please feel free to call me immediately.

Sincerely,

Your Name
Address
City, State Zip Code
Phone:
Fax:
Email:

ESI Debt Validation Letter

Your Name
Address
City, State, Zip Code

Name of Third Party Collector:
Address
City, State, Zip Code

Date

RE: Third Party Collector
    Account No.:_____

Dear Collection Agency,

I am in receipt of my credit bureau report and have noticed that is inaccurate reporting thereon from your company. Pursuant to the **Fair Debt Collection Practices Act, Title 15, Section 1681g, and Fair Credit Reporting Act, Title 15, Section 1592**, I hereby dispute the debt and respectfully request the name and address of the original creditor and any contractual agreement bearing my signature to incur this debt. **I AM ALSO RESPECTFULLY REQUESTING ANY ASSIGNMENTS OF THIS DEBT.**

Please be advised that if this account was initiated via the Internet or telephone, I have a duty to request and you have a duty to disclose responsive electronic evidence. On December 1, 2006, changes relating to **electronically stored information (ESI)** in the **Federal Rules of Civil Procedure** took effect. The changes to Rules 16, 26, 33, 34, 37, 45 and Form 35 provide mandates to the preservation, discoverability, production, accessibility, and costs associated with ESI which includes e-mail, spreadsheets, word processing documents, audio, video, or any content in a digital format.

Therefore, you are required to produce electronic or audio evidence via thumb drive, CD-ROM, or other format, of any electronic evidence which would substantiate when the debt was initiated.

I thank you in advance for your time and attention to this matter.

Kindly,

Your Name
Address
City, State, Zip Code

Certified Mail/Return Receipt

No.:_____

CHAPTER 4
<u>Techniques to Narrow the Production Scope</u>

If you have ever been engaged in litigation, you know that it is a time consuming effort. Once the complaint is filed, the opposing party is on guard to protect the interests of their client. This will include defending against ESI discovery. Some of the main protections to be employed against your request for the production of electronically stored information will include:

- **Challenges to the scope of discovery**
- **The discovery requests are too burdensome**
- **The discovery requests are not relevant**
- **The discovery requests are overbroad**
- **The discovery sought is inaccessible**
- **Challenges to sampling**

There are techniques that can be deployed to minimize the effect of the above challenges and limit the amount of ESI to be produced, reduce costs, and narrow the scope of discovery.

One thing I would do is **narrow the subject matter of the request to the specific claims or defenses of the case**. If your case is in regards to employment discrimination that had resulted in termination based upon an event that had occurred on a specific date, narrow the production request to the date that the event claims to have occurred, and request the electronic database information from the employers' human resources database.

If there was a specific individual who had claimed to have had the authority to terminate based upon an incident or several incidents, then, **limit the scope of discovery to that specific individual**.

Don't forget to **request load files with metadata**! If you are collecting data in an electronic format, you will need to request metadata to be included so that you can determine when the file was created, by whom, and where. That way, you can check that database information with the human resources department to be sure that the HR files are complete and accurate.

Finally, **reach an agreement with opposing counsel as to what ESI is "not reasonably accessible".** By doing so, you take away that protection and have an agreement in writing as to what ESI will and will not be produced.

QUESTIONS IN PREPARATION FOR RULE 26(f) CONFERENCE

1. What are the issues in the case?
2. Who are the key players in the case?
3. Who are the persons most knowledgeable about ESI systems?
4. What events and intervals are relevant?
5. When did preservation duties and privileges attach?
6. What steps have been or will be taken to preserve ESI?
7. Has a Litigation Hold taken place.   If so, when?
8. What third parties hold information that must be preserved, and who will notify them?
9. What metadata is relevant, and how will it be preserved, extracted and produced?
10. What are the data retention policies and practices?
11. What are the backup practices, and what tape archives exist?
12. Are there legacy systems to be addressed?
13. How will the parties handle voice mail, instant messaging and other challenging ESI?
14. Is there a preservation duty going forward, and how will it be met?
15. Is a preservation or protective order needed?
16. Will paper documents be scanned, at what resolution and with what OCR and metadata?
17. What search techniques will be used to identify responsive or privileged ESI?
18. What forms of production are offered or sought?
19. Will single or multi-page .TIFF;s, .PDF's or other image formats be produced?
20. Will load files accompany document images, and how will they be populated?
21. Will there be a need for native file production? Quasi-native production?
22. On what media will ESI be delivered? Optical disks? External drives? Thumb drives?
23. How will we handle inadvertent production of privileged ESI?
24. How will we protect trade secrets and other confidential information in the ESI?
25. How do we resolve questions about printouts before their use in deposition or at trial?
26. How will we handle authentication of the native ESI used in deposition or trial?
27. Who will serve as liaisons or coordinators for each side on ESI issues?
28. Will technical assistants be permitted to communicate directly?
29. Is there a need for an E-Discovery Special Master or Mediator?
30. Can any costs be shared or shifted by agreement?
31. How much time is required to identify, collect, process, review, redact, and produce ESI?
32. When is the next Rule 26(f) Conference (because we need to do this more than once)?

CHAPTER 5
Seven Deadly Sins of the Rule 26(f) "Meet-and-Confer" Conference

Okay, you made it through the trenches. Now, you are at the stage where you have received a Rules 16/26 Proposed Scheduling Order with a Discovery Conference set for a date specified. The court will issue an order which demands that the parties to the action confer and jointly develop a scheduling order and discovery plan containing deadlines and limitations. Thus, it is now time to "Meet-and-Confer".

Federal Rules of Civil Procedure 26(f) requires parties in litigation to "...confer as soon as practicable...[and to]...state the parties' views and proposals on...any issues about disclosure or discovery of electronically stored information..." You need to be sure that you properly handle this "meet-and-confer" session about electronically stored information in order to put yourself in position to effectively negotiate a resolution on the matter at hand. Let's face it, approximately 95% of all cases in litigation do not make it to trial. They are settled using some form of ADR (Alternative Dispute Resolution), i.e., mediation, arbitration, conciliation, negotiation. In fact, most state and federal local rules require that cases be referred to mediation or arbitration, before formal litigation. And, Rule 68 of the Federal Rules of Civil Procedure, enacted in 1938, and state counterparts, give the party who is defending a claim the opportunity to settle by making a formal offer of judgment.

The party who rejects the settlement offer is liable for sanctions if final judgment is not "more favorable" than the settlement offer.

If the amount of any final judgment is less than the settlement offer, after monetary calculations, the prevailing party is required to pay all "costs incurred after the making of the offer." So, as you can see, you should always be thinking about putting yourself in the best possible position for settlement during the discovery process. With that being said, let's talk about the seven deadly sins of the Rule 26(f) "meet-and-confer" and how to minimize e-discovery costs and risks to make sure you will be able to get the data you need from the opposition.

The contents of the seven deadly sins is taken from "Bill Hamilton's Seven Deadly Sins of the Rule 26(f) 'Meet-and-Confer' Conference", published by Bill Hamilton, Dean of the Bryan University E-Discovery Project Management Program, and partner at Quarles & Brady, and Chairman of the Association of Certified E-Discovery Specialists (ACEDS), www.aceds.org., the member organization for professionals in the private and public sectors who work in the field of e-discovery.

I consider Dean Hamilton to be my mentor and he has stated that if you avoid the **Seven Deadly Sins of the Rule 26(f) conference**, you will be well on your way to making e-discovery work for your case.

Deadly Sin #1: Failure to Set the Agenda. Set the agenda means to come prepared to the Rule 26(f) conference and make sure the opponent is prepared as well. You can accomplish this by sending a "Data Preservation Letter" early in the litigation process. The letter will intimate what you expect to accomplish at the conference, what information you will bring to the conference, and what information you expect from the opposition.

Deadly Sin #2: Failure to Manage Preservation. Again, be sure to communicate what you need as far as data in the "Data Preservation Letter". Disclose your preservation decisions early on and be prepared to explain why you have chosen to do so. Demand the same from your opponent. Their data is part of your case and you need to make sure it is secured.

Deadly Sin #3: Failure to Corral E-Discovery and Limit and Phase E-Discovery. Remember, e-discovery is determined by the importance of the data to the case, and the dollar value in proportion to the case. Present a sensible plan to corral the important data. Only a handful of documents are likely to be used at trial, mediation or arbitration. Suggest starting with two or three key employees and build from there. If the question is in regards to discrimination in the workplace which had resulted in termination, start with the names of the presumptive custodians of the HR data and build from there. Reach agreement on a flexible, rolling e-discovery plan for the continued production of documents as you uncover additional parties that may have signed documents on behalf of HR.

Deadly Sin #4: Failure to Set Search Expectations. Make sure that you insist on search quality and demonstrable, statistically valid recall. High recall means the search is pulling most, if not all, the responsive documents. Don't let the opposition test for precision and not test for recall. In a foreclosure case, you may not encounter questions of precision and recall, and if you are a consumer working on a large scale e-discovery case, contact me for further information on precision and recall.

Deadly Sin #5: Failure to Specify the Production Format. Establish the production format in your "Request for Production of Documents". Included in this digital textbook is a format on how to request documents to include load files with metadata. If a third party vendor is to be used, get the vendor's delivery specifications and provide it early to the opposition. Don't let the opposition decide what format is reasonably useable for the case.

Deadly Sin #6: Failure to Protect Against Privilege Waiver from Inadvertent Production. Let's face it...mistakes happen. And, they will happen during the production of documents. If you are a consumer working a large scale e-discovery case, be sure to get the entry of a court order, under Federal Rules of Evidence 502, protecting you against inadvertent disclosure of privileged documents and providing that any determination of non-waiver arising from an inadvertent production is also binding on state court proceedings. Negotiate a written protocol with the opposition as to the procedures to be followed if a privileged document is discovered to have been inadvertently produced.

Deadly Sin #7: Failure to Document. If at all possible, hire a mediator to facilitate any e-discovery disputes. That way, the mediator can draft a "Memorandum of Understanding" and memorialize the conference as you would a settlement agreement or contract. Mediation of ESI disputes is a growing field in the world of e-discovery as data is becoming more abundant. Don't let what you have accomplished at the Rule 26(f) get lost along the road to success.

Follow these steps and you will have a successful Rule 26(f) and a complete and accurate Proposed Scheduling Order. For course information about statistical sampling, search and recall, contact Dean Hamilton at william.hamilton@bryanuniversity.edu. For further consultation on Rule 26(f) preparation and planning for an imminent, pending, or impending foreclosure, contact eDiscovery Solutions, Inc. at 888-502-0586, or ajohnson@ediscoverynow.net.

Chapter 6
Rule 26(f) Conference Preparation

Okay, you've filed an answer to the complaint, requested your first set of interrogatories, ESI interrogatories, expert witness interrogatories, and request for production of documents to include load files with metadata. Now, you should be prepared to meet with the opposing party and speak intelligently about the nature and extent of potentially relevant ESI. We will examine some questions that should be addressed and illuminate the reasons why these questions should be asked and answered, BEFORE the Rule 26(f) Conference:

1. What are the issues in the case? The parties should be on the page as to what the issues are so that there are no objections as to the preservation and production of relevant ESI.
2. Who are the key players in the case? Identifying the key custodians is critical to uncovering who have relevant ESI.
3. Who are the persons most knowledgeable about ESI systems? You will need to communicate with someone who can describe the network infrastructure and organization of ESI, including locations of user files and storage areas, as well as file servers, email servers, application servers, and web servers.
4. What events and intervals are relevant? Narrowing down the relevant time frame is essential to narrowing the scope of relevant ESI.
5. When did preservation duties and privileges attach? You want to investigate and find out whether a formal Litigation Hold has been implemented. Remember, the party initiating the litigation has a duty to preserve ESI much earlier than the responding party.
6. What steps have been or will be taken to preserve ESI? In addition to uncovering whether a formal Litigation Hold has been implemented, you will also want to know whether there is a

written records retention/destruction policy, and if so, has the data destruction and auto-deletion policies have been suspended.

7. What third parties hold information that must be preserved, and who will notify them? This is especially important in workplace conflict or employment discrimination cases because there may be more than one person with authority to hire and fire as well as more than one person with HR access to your files.

8. What forms of production are offered or sough? Will the opposing party produce the documents in native file format? .TIFF? Will the data be provided on a CD-ROM? Flash drive? Paper format?

9. What ESI will be claimed as not reasonably accessible, and on what basis? This is an important inquiry because you can narrow your scope of what ESI is relevant and if the other side objects, you can ask why and have a meeting of the minds to ascertain what is reasonably accessible and what is not.

10.   When is the next Rule 26(f) Conference (because you will need to do this more than once).

For somewhat different approaches to the E-Discovery topics to be addressed at a Rule 26(f) Conference, be sure to visit the discussion of Magistrate Judge Paul W. Grimm at:
www.mdd.uscourts.gov/news/news/ESIProtocol.pdf.

Sample Rule 26(f) Outline

(To Be Used for Preparing Joint Scheduling Report)

According to Rule 26(f) of the Federal Rules of Civil Procedure, the parties in litigation "must confer as soon as practicable..." in efforts to "...consider the nature and basis of their claims and defenses and the possibilities for promptly settling or resolving the case; make or arrange for the disclosures required by Rule 26(a)(1); discuss any issues about preserving discoverable information; and develop a proposed discovery plan."

This Rule 26(f) Outline will illuminate what I would plan to disclose.

YOUR CASE

1. What changes are to be made with respect to the timing, form, or requirement for disclosures under Rule 26(a), including a statement of when the initial disclosures were made or will be made.

   a. Time is of the essence, so it would be critical that my case would act immediately to preserve ESI since electronic information can be easily destroyed, concealed, altered, or protected;

   b. The form of disclosure would include requests for paper documents, recorded information, electronic data and documents, including but not limited to desktop and laptop computers, network servers, email servers, handheld devices, storage devices including CD's and ZIP drives, offsite storage, and remote computers with network connections.

2. The subjects on which discovery may be needed. This would include:

a. Narrowing the subject matter of the request to the specific claims or defenses of the case;

b. Limiting discovery to specific individuals, departments or organizations;

c. Setting forth a time period for the information requested by the opposing party;

d. Limitation of the search to specific types of files, i.e., email, word processing, databases, paper documents (letters);

e. An attempt to reach an agreement on specific search terms to use on the collected data, because it would be reasonable to conclude that the resulting volume of ESI will determine the costs of the review;

f. Consideration of sampling of the data in question to determine relevancy and burdensome issues;

g. Obtaining an agreement with respect to confidential, proprietary, or privileged information;

h. Collection of discoverable information in an electronic format in efforts to reduce costs;

i. Discussion as to whether metadata will be processed, reviewed, and disclosed;

j. Agreement on the criteria to be used when de-duping ESI;

k. Agreement on what ESI will be marked as "not reasonably accessible."

3. Issues about disclosure or discovery of ESI, including the form or forms in which it should be produced. This would include:

a. Native files—copies of the original documents in the format created by the authorizing application, i.e., .doc, .xls, etc.

b. Near native files—may include many different types of files and may also include electronically converted, searchable PDF's;

    c. Near paper files—would include files that cannot be searched or indexed, and sometimes those that can, i.e., TIFF, PDF;

    d. Paper files—docs that had originated in paper form or digital files that have been printed to paper.

4. Issues about claims of privilege or of protection as trial-preparation materials, including who would be responsible for reviewing documents for production and assertion of privileges. This would include issues pertaining to:

    a. Admissibility of electronic evidence, e.g., is the evidence relevant, and not substantially outweighed by the danger of prejudice? (FRE 401-404);

    b. Is there sufficient evidence for the court to grant preliminary admission of evidence? (FRE 104)

    c. Can the evidence be authenticated properly? (FRE 901)

    d. Is the evidence hearsay and not subject to an exception? (FRE 801-803)

    e. Does the "Best Evidence Rule" require the original of the document to be produced? (FRE 1001-1003)

    f. Is it necessary to have an expert witness testify or to use a lay witness' testimony to present the computer results? (FRE 702-705)

5. What changes should be made in the limitations on discovery imposed under Rule 26(f) or by local rule, and what other limitations should be imposed; and

6. Any other orders that the court should issue under Rule 269c) or under Rule 16(b) and (c).

OPPOSING PARTY CASE

1. What changes are to be made with respect to the timing, form, or requirement for disclosures under Rule 26(a), including a statement of when the initial disclosures were made or will be made.

    a. Time is of the essence, so it would be critical that the opposing party would act immediately to preserve ESI since electronic information can be easily destroyed, concealed, altered, or protected;

    b. The form of disclosure would include requests for paper documents, recorded information, electronic data and documents, including but not limited to desktop and laptop computers, network servers, email servers, handheld devices, storage devices including CD's and ZIP drives, offsite storage, and remote computers with network connections.

2. The subjects on which discovery may be needed. This would include:

    a. Narrowing the subject matter of the request to the specific claims or defenses of the case;

    b. Limiting discovery to specific individuals, departments or organizations;

    c. Setting forth a time period for the information requested by the opposing party;

    d. Limitation of the search to specific types of files, i.e., email, word processing, databases, paper documents (letters);

    e. An attempt to reach an agreement on specific search terms to use on the collected data, because it would be reasonable to conclude that the resulting volume of ESI will determine the costs of the review;

    f.   Consideration of sampling of the data in question to determine relevancy and burdensome issues;

    g.   Obtaining an agreement with respect to confidential, proprietary, or privileged information;

    h.   Collection of discoverable information in an electronic format in efforts to reduce costs;

    i.   Discussion as to whether metadata will be processed, reviewed, and disclosed;

    j.   Agreement on the criteria to be used when de-duping ESI;

    k.   Agreement on what ESI will be marked as "not reasonably accessible."

3. Issues about disclosure or discovery of ESI, including the form or forms in which it should be produced. This would include:

    a.   Native files—copies of the original documents in the format created by the authorizing application, i.e., .doc, .xls, etc.

    b.   Near native files—may include many different types of files and may also include electronically converted, searchable PDF's;

    c.   Near paper files—would include files that cannot be searched or indexed, and sometimes those that can, i.e., TIFF, PDF;

    d.   Paper files—docs that had originated in paper form or digital files that have been printed to paper.

4. Issues about claims of privilege or of protection as trial-preparation materials, including who would be responsible for reviewing documents for production and assertion of privileges. This would include issues pertaining to:

a. Admissibility of electronic evidence, e.g., is the evidence relevant, and not substantially outweighed by the danger of prejudice? (FRE 401-404);

b. Is there sufficient evidence for the court to grant preliminary admission of evidence? (FRE 104)

c. Can the evidence be authenticated properly? (FRE 901)

d. Is the evidence hearsay and not subject to an exception? (FRE 801-803)

e. Does the "Best Evidence Rule" require the original of the document to be produced? (FRE 1001-1003)

f. Is it necessary to have an expert witness testify or to use a lay witness' testimony to present the computer results? (FRE 702-705)

5. What changes should be made in the limitations on discovery imposed under Rule 26(f) or by local rule, and what other limitations should be imposed; and

6. Any other orders that the court should issue under Rule 269c) or under Rule 16(b) and (c).

By:

Chapter 7
<u>The E-Discovery Budget</u>

In an identity theft case, as well as others, there will be a request for the production of documents. The opposing party will claim that the discovery requests are burdensome, not relevant, overbroad, accessible, and beyond the scope of the litigation. So you, the consumer, will have to narrow the scope and request the most relevant documents to be produced, which in a wrongful termination situation, would only be a few documents, i.e., emails, notes of phone calls or messages, notes about meetings, performance reviews, pay raises, witnesses, just to name a few.

Therefore, in an identity theft situation, as well as other cases, there will not be more than 7 +/- 2 documents to be requested, which is all that the human mind can focus on at any one time, anyway. George A. Miller, a cognitive psychologist, has suggested that 7 +/- 2 is the magic number that characterizes people's memory performance on random lists of letters, words, numbers, etc. His theory is known as "Miller's Law". Miller's Law is a legal art of persuasion and limitations on information transmission on the premise that no juror can possibly hold more than 5 to 9 documents in their head at a time. Seven is the magic number and when you think about, it really makes sense. Most of what we have become accustomed to realizing every day comes in sevens:

- **Seven wonders of the world**
- **Seven seas**
- **Seven deadly sins**
- **Seven daughters of Atlas in the Pleiades**
- **Seven ages of man**
- **Seven primary colors**

- **Seven notes of a musical scale**
- **Seven days of the week**

For larger e-discovery projects there will be serious budget implications to consider at each stage of the e-discovery project lifecycle. This lifecycle includes: initiation, planning, execution, monitoring & control, and closure. Each of these stages are further illuminated as follows:

- **Initiation:** Initial budget assessments typically used for scope management and negotiation with adversaries
- **Planning:** Early analysis of objective, requirements, assumptions and scope enables accurate planning of expenses
- **Execution:** Sound budgeting ensures that financial resources are available when needed and avoids unpleasant surprises as work is performed
- **Monitoring & Control:** Active monitoring of scope enables anticipation of issues and agile decision making
- **Closure:** Review of actual spend vs. budget for use in planning future e-discovery efforts

E-Discovery Budget Development Process

During the "initiation" phase, you would want to discuss the case matter with the case team, review court documents, past work for client, and similar cases for other clients as part of your due diligence.

Also, as part of the due diligence, you would want to determine the scope of the project, "meet and confer" as often as possible, conduct initial custodian interviews, and conduct IT interviews along with data mapping.

Next, you would want to develop initial assumptions about the project and find out how many custodians there are, data volumes, reduction percentages, document counts, quality control estimates, production volume, and costs & fees.

Then, create an initial budget. Combine the requirements and initial assumptions into preliminary budget.

Finally, monitor & refine all of the above and integrate any new information (revised assumptions, fees, etc.) into the budget. You will also monitor ongoing activities for budget conformance and make adjustments as necessary.

Remember, the above guidelines are to be used for e-discovery projects involving multiple gigabytes of data. You will need to examine your source gigabyte total which is the combined volume (in GB) to be collected from all custodians BEFORE any data reduction operations are performed. (Source GB Total = Estimated number of custodians X estimated GB per custodian)

For e-discovery projects that are small in nature, i.e., involving less than 50-100 documents to be produced, you will not need to examine any source GB total because the data will not be voluminous. In a wrongful termination situation, you will only need to obtain a few documents relating to the circumstances surrounding the termination. As you can see, there is not very much data to be ascertained.

Whether you are in a large or small e-discovery situation, Miller's Law will still come into play so you will need to keep that in mind as you request the production of documents. No jury will be able to hold more than 5 to 9 documents or pieces of evidence in their head at one time.

If you are a consumer working a small scale e-discovery project and would like more information about how to develop and manage an e-discovery budget, contact eDiscovery Solutions, Inc. at 888-502-0586, or email at ajohnson@ediscoverynow.net.

SAMPLE

E-DISCOVERY BUDGET MEMORANDUM

Date

TO: E-Discovery Case Team

FROM: Anthony Johnson, E-Discovery Consultant

Re: E-Discovery Budget

E-Discovery Case Team,

Attached please find the proposed e-discovery budget in efforts to substantiate the rationale and process in support of the upcoming litigation. The figures contained in the budget proposal were not arbitrarily obtained. These figures were acquired after gathering basic information about the litigation, key players involved, potential custodians, types of hardware and software they use, and what kinds of servers on which responsive data may reside.

Please be advised that the amount, types and storage locations of the data can significantly affect costs and, therefore, I have used a high/low range instead of a fixed volume in order to account for any changes that may occur in the initial custodian counts and/or data volumes. It is extremely challenging to estimate data reduction so early in the project, so I would ask that each team member focus on how the data was identified/collected; type of review, and review criteria.

The attached budget estimates will continue to be monitored as the case metastasizes throughout the EDRM lifecycle. Quality Control estimates will be performed to ensure that we are acting in accordance with the budget. As the case metamorphoses into various stages, my confidence level will increase and I am certain that as we amalgamate to the late budget stage, I will have a very high level of confidence that we can and will complete the project on time and within budget.

Please feel free to contact me if you have any questions, comments or concerns about the budget at 888-502-0586, or www.ediscoverynow.net.

Kindly,

Anthony Johnson, E-Discovery Consultant

SAMPLE
E-Discovery Budget Analysis for 25 GB of Data

Let's take a look at an example of the total expenses for E-Discovery for an organization for 25 GB of data:

EDRM Stage	Dollars	Percentage
Collection	$10,000	4%
Processing	$94,000	36%
Review	$153,000	58%
Production	$4,000	2%
Total	$261,000	100%
Total for Review		
And Processing	$247,000	94%

Range of Estimates for Documents per GB of Data

# of Docs	Low	Industry Standard	Medium	High
1 GB	5,000	10,000	15,000	25,000

Rates for Document Review for Attorneys

	Outsource	Low Staff	Medium	High
Hourly Rates	$28/hr.	$40/hr.	$53/hr.	$65/hr.
Price Per Year	$56,000	$80,000	$105,000	$130,000

Rate of Document Review

Docs per 1 GB	5,000	10,000	15,000	25,000
Reviewed per day	400	400	400	400
Days of Review	12.5	25	37.5	62.5

As you can see, litigation preparation for an organization can and will be expensive. One way to reduce the costs associated with processing and reviewing ESI will be to employ "**SAMPLING**".

- **SAMPLING**
  - Allows requesting party to take a snap shot of the producing party's files and draw conclusions of the whole population based on those findings
  - Also allows a party or the court to determine if expensive and costly discovery is likely to lead to relevant information or if the burden to produce outweigh the benefit

Expected Vendor Fees For 1-100 GB of Data

	Low	Average	Medium	High
Price per 1GB	$750	$1,000	$1,200	$1,800
Price 100 GB	$75k	$100k	$120k	$180k

*Using a consumer or litigation assistant to conduct document review is not unauthorized practice of law.

Chapter 8
The E-Discovery Checklist

Checklists are used in every industry known to man. Doctors use them when performing major surgery or a routine examination. Construction contractors use them when building homes. Architects use them to design buildings. In the world of e-discovery for identity theft prevention and protection, a checklist should also be used so that you will not skip or miss any important steps along the way.

Checklists are important because of the fallibility of human memory and attention, especially when it comes to mundane, routine matters that are easily overlooked when compared with more challenging events that may require more focused attention.

DO-CONFIRM vs. READ-DO CHECKLIST

In an organization, when making a checklist, you have a number of key decisions. You must define a clear pause point at which the checklist is supposed to be used, i.e., when litigation is imminent, pending, or impending. You must decide whether you want a **DO-CONFIRM** checklist or **READ-DO** checklist.

With a **DO-CONFIRM** checklist, team members perform their jobs from memory and experience, often separately. But then they stop. They pause to run the checklist and confirm that everything that was supposed to be done was done.

With a **READ-DO** checklist, on the other hand, people carry out the tasks as they check them off, sort of like a recipe. So for any new checklist created from scratch, you have to pick the type that makes the most sense for the situation.

The checklist cannot be lengthy. A rule of thumb some use is to keep it to between five and nine items, which is the limit of working memory. Miller's Law holds that seven plus/minus two (7+/-2) is a *legal art of persuasion* on limitations of information transmission. No jury can possibly hold more than five (5) to nine (9) documents in their head at a time. George A. Miller, (Miler's Law) a cognitive psychologist, has suggested that 7 +/- 2 is the magic number that characterizes people's memory performance on random lists of letters, words, numbers, etc.

However, for an ediscovery checklist to protect you from identity theft and any potential liability, the checklist should be a bit more comprehensive. Once we have identified the relevant data for preservation, collection, processing, review, analysis, and production, we will narrow down the relevant documents for submission to a trier of fact, which will be between five and nine items.

E-DISCOVERY IDENTIFICATION AND PRESERVATION CHECKLIST

In the event that litigation is imminent, pending, or impending, an organization should, at a minimum, employ the following checklist to ensure litigation readiness:

READ-DO CHECKLIST

- What is the relevant time frame?
- Has a formal Litigation Hold been implemented?
- Is there a written records retention/destruction policy?

- Have data destruction and auto-deletion policies been suspended?
- Sources of data containing potentially relevant ESI
- **Network systems**
  - Describe the network infrastructure and organization of ESI including locations of user files and storage areas
  - Are there file servers, email servers, application or web servers?
  - What is the operating system and version?
  - Is this a centralized network system with a data center or separate networks?
- **Email System**
  - What email application and version is currently in use?
  - Has the current email system been in place during the relevant time period?
  - If not, describe prior system _____.
  - How long does active email remain on server?
  - Deletion policy?
  - Is email archived by the user or force archived?
  - Where?_____.
  - Is is necessary to collect archived email?
  - Is there a size limitation on a user account?
  - If yes, what is size limitation?
  - Does blackberry, Apple, or Android email pass through email servers?
  - Is there an email retention/archiving system in place?
  - Name and version of application:_____.
  - When were emails first retained/archived using this system?_____.
- **Local Desktop Workstations**
  - Are PC or laptop workstations in use?

- o If so, type of PC/Laptop and hard drive size:_____.
- o Can users save to local hard drive location?
- o Is the USB, CD/DVD or floppy drive active?
- o Are PC's or laptops ever re-imaged or replaced?
- o Explain:_____.

- **Network Personal Shares**
  - o Does every user have a personal network share?
  - o Should the entire personal share be collected?
  - o If no, specify fires/folders to collect:_____.

- **Network Group Shares**
  - o List the Group shares to collect:_____.
  - o Should the entire group share be collected?
  - o If not, specify folders/files to collect?

- **Databases**
  - o Are there any databases, applications, or proprietary programs that generate or contain potentially relevant ESI?
  - o Name of program or application and format of data:_____.

- **Third Party Providers**
  - o Do any third-party providers for internet, social media, Bloomberg, records management, email routing, etc., have any relevant ESI?
  - o If yes, who and for what and where?

- **Text or Instant Messaging**
  - o Do users have a text message or instant messaging program?

- o Is the data stored or backed up?
- **Telephone Systems (office or cell phone)**
  - o Are voicemail messages within the scope of the case?
  - o If yes, how is data retained?
- **Backup Systems**
  - o Has backup tape rotation been suspended?
  - o Name and type of backup system?
  - o What data is backed up?
  - o Describe the backup process (full, incremental, frequency):_____.
  - o Is backup media available for the relevant time frame?
- **Policy on Former Employees**
  - o Is there a written policy on former employees?
  - o What is the retention/destruction policy for workstation laptop?
  - o Email?
  - o Personal Network Share?
- **System Upgrades – Hardware and Software**
  - o Have there been any upgrades, hardware or software, in the relevant time period or that are planned in the next 12 months that will impact data storage, retention or backup media? Please explain:_____.

- **Legacy Systems**
  - o Are there any legacy systems, old data storage or former applications running which may contain data relevant to this matter?
  - o If yes, what is the data and how is it stored?
  - o Please explain:_____.
- **Paper Documents**
  - o Are there paper documents associated with this case?

- o Is someone gathering paper documents?
- o How many boxes of paper can be expected?
- **Client IT Personnel**
  - o Are client's IT personnel trained in computer forensics?
  - o Is healthcare IT staff able to forensically collect the ESI, including write protected data, maintain chain of custody, document the process and testify, if necessary?

As you can see, the above **READ-DO** checklist must be read, and checked off, line by line, to ensure an appropriate litigation readiness program in an organization. If you would employ this initial checklist for Identification and Preservation of ESI, you will be on your way to ensuring compliance with any court order or exchange of information during discovery in the event your organization would come under fire.

There is also an ***ESI Collection Checklist***.

An ***ESI Processing Specification Checklist***.

An ***ESI Production Specification Checklist***.

A ***Document Retention Log***.

A ***Data Collection Log***.

And, a ***Chain of Custody Form***.

All to ensure an organization's litigation readiness and compliance.

RECAP OF A CONSUMER'S ROLE

1. A consumer trained in e-discovery should identify who is available to participate in the e-discovery project.
2. A consumer trained in e-discovery should provide all relevant or applicable discovery requests, objections, responses, motion to compel with exhibits, motions for protective order with exhibits, applicable discovery orders, and Rule 26 Scheduling Orders.
3. If requests can be grouped by issue, a consumer skilled in e-discovery should identify the issue and the position his client takes with respect to that issue.
4. A consumer skilled in e-discovery should be prepared to discuss in confidence a general overview of the client's data mapping. (Data mapping traces the connection from the communicator and the methodology of the communication)
5. A consumer skilled in e-discovery should identify whether any spoliation pitfalls exist, articulate any relevant time issues, identify any known cost or burden concerns, and identify any privilege concerns.
6. A consumer skilled in e-discovery should discuss any issues relating to the compatibility and/or capability to produce electronic information from the client, to the responding law firm to opposing counsel or opposing law firm.
7. If the consumer skilled in e-discovery is aware of any electronic information that has been requested that the consumer believes is relevant, but the information is reasonably inaccessible, the consumer should identify the information and explain why the information is inaccessible.
8. Searches must be conducted to identify and retrieve discoverable information. (Most commonly, searches for emails and/or voicemails are requested, for example. For different types of data, counsel should identify keywords or search terms the

consumer believes are reasonably calculated to identify relevant information)
9. The consumer skilled in e-discovery should be prepared to discuss what format the information is requested, i.e., native file format, etc.

*Note: Within this Checklist would be a "sub-checklist" to check off and follow the e-discovery forms that must be addressed.

Chapter 9
<u>Five Secrets of Search</u>

Okay. You've made it to the point of negotiating which documents will be relevant or not and have the other side to the table to listen to what is important to the case. You've also effectively employed the Seven Deadly Sins of the Rule 26(f) Conference and have managed to put yourself in a position to conduct a search of relevant ESI. Employ these search secrets and you will be on your way to effectively corralling relevant electronic documents.

1st SEARCH SECRET: *Keywords Search* is remarkably ineffective at recall. What is recall? Recall is the percentage of documents (hot documents) that are responsive divided by the number of responsive documents. The "hot documents" are those that are reflected in your list of key words. We use recall with precision, and precision is the number of documents responsive divided by the number of documents that are a hit. Therefore, keyword search alone only catches 20% of relevant evidence in a large, complex dataset, such as an email collection. And, keyword search only provides reliable recall value when used as part of a multi-model process that uses other search methods and quality controls, such as interactive testing, sampling, and adjustments. However, keyword search is still a viable tool when used with predictive coding, a process embedded in software.

How does predictive coding work? Persons knowledgeable about a matter, typically a lawyer or case manager, will identify a small number of documents that are representative of the categories to be reviewed and coded (i.e., relevance, responsiveness, privilege, issue-relation).

The Case Manager will then use sophisticated search and analytical tools, including keyword, Boolean, and concept search, concept grouping, and more than 40+ automatically populated filters— referred to as "Predictive Analytics" to identify probative documents for each category to be reviewed and coded.

Next, the Case Manager then obtains a small set of documents into a relevant category and starts the process by where the system uses each seed set to identify and prioritize all substantially similar documents over the complete corpus.

Subsequently, the Case Manager and review team (if any) will then review and code all computer suggested documents to ensure their proper categorization and further calibrate the system.

The final step is to employ "Predictive Sampling" methodology to ensure accuracy and completeness of predictive coding process, referred to as *precision and recall*. (*See*, **Da Silva Moore**, SDNY, Feb. 12, 2012, Magistrate Judge Peck issued judicial authority for "predictive coding").

TAKE-AWAY: Keyword search alone is ineffective because of:

- **Word and phrase variations**
- **Mispelllings**
- **Abbreves**
- **Slang**
- **Obtusity**

*When large data sets are involved, no human is smart enough to guess the right keywords.

2nd SEARCH SECRET: *Human Review* is not the gold standard either. Humans are very poor at making relevancy determinations about data sets (in large data sets). However, humans can agree and create a gold standard if relevance is defined clearly enough to reviewers—and—if objective mistakes by reviewers (as opposed to subjective disagreements) are identified and corrected.

TAKE-AWAY: There is a triple-pass solution to human review:

- **One lawyer can express his views on relevance**
- **Opposing counsel, uses independent judgment to either agree or disagree, i.e., object**
- **Third expert, a judge or mediator, can hear arguments from both sides then make a final determination**

3rd SEARCH SECRET: *Team Approach* where humans use machines in nonlinear function, i.e., to conduct a final check of computer for classifications like privilege before production. This will improve review team quality by catching random errors of inattention, while second review by an authoritative reviewer can correct misconceptions of relevance during the review process, and adjust for errors once it is complete. By utilizing this team review approach, one can exclude reviewers whose proportion relevance are significantly different from the median, and re-apportion their work to the more reliable reviewers.

TAKE-AWAY: Quantify the trade-off between manual effort and automation, and validate protocols for verifying the correctness of either approach in practice, are relevant in the multi-stage, hybrid work flows of contemporary legal review and production.

Case Issues:

- **Relevancy**
- **Privilege**
- **Confidentiality**
- **Categorization, i.e., Issue Tagging**
  - **Issue Tagging must be kept simple and straightforward**
  - **Reviewers need subject matter expertise**

4TH SEARCH SECRET: *Relevant is Irrelevant.* Merely relevant documents in big data reviews are irrelevant as compared to highly relevant documents. That is because merely relevant documents will not be admissible into evidence!

*The gathering of evidence for admission at trial is, after all, the only valid purpose of discovery!

**Also, discovery is only permitted for purposes of preparation for trial. It is never permitted to extort one side into a settlement to avoid the costs of a document review, or to at least gain a strategic edge, although we all know this happens all the time!

TAKE-AWAY: Merely relevant evidence = waste of time and inadmissible. See, Rule 403 of Federal Evidence Code.

- Rule 403. Excluding relevant evidence for prejudice, confusion, waste of time, or other reasons.
- Rule 611. "The Court shall exercise reasonable control over...presenting evidence so as to...(2) avoid wasting time..."

- Rule 26(b)(2)(C)(i). Balancing tests. Benefits and burdens of discovery.
- New e-discovery Rule 26(b)(2)(B). Balancing test for hard-to-access ESI.
- Rule 26(g). Requires only a reasonable inquiry of completeness in a response to discovery.
- Rule 26(g)(1)(B). Prohibits any request for discovery made "for any improper purpose, such as to harass, cause unnecessary delay, or needlessly increase the cost of litigation" and prohibits any request that is unreasonable or unduly burdensome or expensive "considering the needs of the case, prior discovery in the case, the amount in controversy, and the importance of the issues at stake in the action.

*Rules clearly state that cumulative evidence is not, or at least should not, be subject to discovery.

- **Rule 1. FRCP requires all other rules to be interpreted and applied so as to make litigation just, speedy, and inexpensive.**

5th SEARCH SECRET: *Magic Power of 7 +/- 2.* Seven plus/minus 2 should control all e-discovery. Think about this for a second and ask yourself, what is the purpose of a trial?

- **To persuade**
- **Use an even playing field**
- **Determine what had happened and what should be done about it**

Seven plus/minus 2 (7+/-2) is a *legal art of persuasion* on limitations of information transmission. No jury can possibly hold more than five (5) to nine (9) documents in their head at a time. George A.

Miller, (Miler's Law) a cognitive psychologist, has suggested that 7 +/- 2 is the magic number that characterizes people's memory performance on random lists of letters, words, numbers, etc. Let's take a moment to think about the magic number of seven (again):

- **Seven wonders of the world**
- **Seven seas**
- **Seven deadly sins**
- **Seven daughters of Atlas in the Pleiades**
- **Seven ages of man**
- **Seven primary colors**
- **Seven notes of musical scale**
- **Seven days of the week**

TAKE-AWAY: Use Miller's Law as your guide when moving through the EDRM to determine what relevant evidence to present to a fact-finder.

RECAP: If you were to employ these five search secrets you will save yourselves valuable time and money during litigation. Remember, 1 gigabyte of data is equivalent to one pickup truck of paper documents and can cost from $10,000 to $20,000 to review manually.

Therefore, if you were to manually review 100 documents per hour, and 1 gigabyte of date equals 30 big boxes of papers, each box would hold 3,000 pages. If each document file in the box is 100 pages, then, the box would hold 300 documents of files. If you are paying a healthcare IT professional as part of your legal team to review these documents, it would take about 90 hours or two weeks to review these documents. At $200 per hour, times 90 hours, this would equal a whopping $18,000! ($200 x 90 = $18,000) And, five (5) gigabytes of data is standard in any medical malpractice suit.

Chapter 10
Putting It All Together

Electronic data is here to stay. Also, identity theft is here and will continue to metamorphose into new types, whether high tech or low tech. Emails, text messages, word processing documents all are a way of life. Thus, it is important to understand the nuts and bolts of electronic data, or "e-discovery" not only in a professional sense, but also for a better understanding of the management of data that is created daily.

For more information on E-Discovery for consumers and financial institutions for identity theft prevention and protection, including a step-by-step instructional Training Webinar which will include:

- **The Electronic Discovery Identification and Preservation Questionnaire**
- **ESI Collection Specification**
- **ESI Processing Specification**
- **ESI Production Specification**
- **Data Collection Log**
- **Document Collection Log**
- **Sample Request for Interrogatories—Admissions**
- **Sample Request for ESI Interrogatories**
- **Sample Request for Expert Witness Interrogatories**
- **Sample Request for Production of Documents to Include Load Files with Metadata**
- **Litigation Hold Notice**
- **Cloud-based ESI**

Contact Anthony Johnson, eDiscovery Solutions, Inc. at
888-502-0586 or visit www.ediscoverynow.net,
email: ajohnson@ediscoverynow.net.

ACKNOWLEDGEMENTS

First and foremost, I'd like to thank William "Bill" Hamilton, Executive Director, University of Florida E-Discovery Project; Partner, Quarles & Brady LLP; and Dean of the Department of E-Discovery Project Management at Bryan University. I consider Bill to be my mentor in all matters regarding e-discovery and life. His knowledge and skills in the area of electronic discovery and evidence is second to none and in my opinion is considered the "Godfather" of e-discovery.

Next, I'd like to thank George Socha, Co-Founder, EDRM; and President, Socha Consulting, LLC. I have had the pleasure of meeting George at The University of Florida Levin College of Law and EDRM Conference on E-Discovery for the Small and Medium Case, on April 4-5, 2013. George has inspired me to think outside the box and apply the concepts of his EDRM to another form of e-discovery to be introduced in the coming weeks.

I'd like to thank Michael R. Arkfeld and his series of Arkfeld's Best Practices Guide for E-Discovery. The "Best Practices" series is on point with a step-by-step analysis of what e-discovery is and how to effectively utilized e-discovery for a small, medium, or large case.

I'd also like to thank Browning E. Marean (RIP) for publishing his "Electronic Discovery and Records Management Guide: Rules, Checklists, and Forms", 2011-2012 Edition. I use this guide on a daily basis as I am constantly looking for ways to be more efficient in the world of e-discovery.

Special thanks must be given to Bryan University and the E-Discovery Project Management graduate diploma course. The course was challenging and rewarding and has certainly taken my entrepreneurial vision to a new level. The staff and professors are highly skilled professionals and very knowledgeable in the world of e-discovery and I need to take a moment to personally acknowledge them all:

- **William "Bill" Hamilton, Dean and Instructor, EDIS 500 & 512**
- **Dr. Kris Ewell, Instructor, EDIS 501**
- **Helen Bergman Moure, Instructor, EDIS 502**
- **Cecil Lynn, Instructor, EDIS 511**
- **Joel Wuesthoff, Instructor, EDIS 513**
- **Wendy Axelrod, Instructor, EDIS 521**
- **Dera Nevin, Instructor, EDIS 522**
- **Mike Quartararo, Instructor, E-Discovery Labs, EDIS 555 & 599**
- **Gary Salazar, IT, Bryan University**
- **Jerome Guidetta, Recruiter, Bryan University**

Also, special thanks the Wall Street Journal (WSJ). For me, the WSJ is the best newspaper in the world. It kept me in the loop as I researched identity theft for the idea and concept of this book.

The USA Today. Another great source of information. Truly invaluable and challenged me daily to stay with the concept and follow the trends of identity theft crisis around the county.

Rolling Stone Magazine. The November 25, 2010 article written by Matt Taibbi inspired this story.

TIME Magazine. The November 29, 2010 article written by Stephen Gandel helped shed more light on the mortgage foreclosure crisis, as well as consumer debt issues.

Fareed Zakaria GPS. This show, which airs on CNN on Sunday morning and afternoon, is my favorite, and always cover the issues that matters most in our lives.

Joel Greenblatt's, "You Can Be A Stock Market Genius." Greenblatt's book illuminated how to pick stocks based upon "extraordinary corporate events." The book also opened my eyes as to how to ascertain information about securities offerings by searching sec.gov and EDGAR, the financial reporting websites, which is where securitization of investment trusts must keep filings. If it were not for this book, I would not have been able to write intelligently about trusts as they relate to the assignment of debt or articulate identity theft as it relates to asset backed securities.

Michael Lewis, the author of "Liar's Poker" and "The Big Short." Both books contributed to my knowledge and insight about how the mortgage bond market works, including the use of synthetic subprime mortgage bond-backed CDO's and credit default swaps, knowledge necessary to understand consumer-related issues, because consumer debt, just like mortgages, are transferred and assigned as asset-backed securities.

"60 Minutes." The best news magazine on television bar none. The 2010 interview with Michael Burry piqued my interest into learning more about the mortgage industry and prompted me to purchase Michael Lewis's "The Big Short." Also, Scott Pelley's report, "The Next Housing Shock," which aired on April 3, 2011, confirmed what I had written about the foreclosure crisis and has acted as a catalyst for me to become a consumer advocate and traverse into consumer debt issues.

The Financial Times. This newspaper has given me the global perspective of the world's financial crisis, broadened my horizons, and punctuated the importance of looking at any crisis of our times with a global eye.

Finally, thanks must be given to anyone and everyone who has contributed to my growth and development over the past decade, which has made this book possible, especially Gokhan Ozturk "Dr. Oz" of Canada via Turkish decent, who suggested that I write a book about the mortgage foreclosure crisis. Our "pow-wows" about the crisis played a significant part in motivating me to become an author.

"Big Hand", Sylvester Fair, who kept me focused on the task at hand notwithstanding the challenges we faced on a daily basis.

Shannon Henderson, another of my favorite persons to "pow-wow" with about the world as we saw it and how we could someday make a difference. I appreciate your thoughtful insight about your vision of the world.

"B-Man" Bryce Rowell, who, like Dr. Oz, Big Hand, and Shannon Henderson, have kept me grounded in my quest to make the best of any situation and make the world a better place. I thank you for your thought-provoking mind and genius on the issues of the day.

Francisco and Clady Martinez, whom I cannot say enough about. Your time and attention to my needs inspired me to do more, be more, become more.

Pierre Sellan, an inspiration to endure even during the tough times. Your words of encouragement still resonate with me.

Ravanna Thomas-El, my long-time childhood friend. I look forward to our daily pow-wows and your intellectual prowess is always welcome. I couldn't have done this 16th book on the "crisis of the day" that affect our lives without your input and encouragement.

Earl Williams, whom like all of the above, has given me "straight talk" about the crisis illuminating my conscience on a daily basis. I appreciate your time and energy to listen to my thoughts as I wrestled with the crisis of the day that affect our lives.

Rolesha Brown, my classmate at Bryan University's prestigious E-Discovery Project Management Graduate Program. It was tough learning the nuances of electronically stored information ("ESI"), but we made it! I appreciate your time, assistance, dedication, and patience with me in helping me to understand binary code at the level of instruction at the university. Your belief in me and my goals will payoff ten-fold as I prepare to launch the IPO of eDiscovery Solutions, Inc. in the coming year.

Special thanks to Candace Stone who believed in me and my work to invite me to a book signing conference she was hosting in Atlanta,

GA in 2012. Although I did not attend for reasons beyond my control, I appreciate your vision, genius, and gracious spirit to believe that people change, the world is fluid, not static, and we all deserve an opportunity to make a contribution to society.

Last but not least, Darren Keys, a standup guy, who not only has endured the crisis of the day, but has come out on top and has mastered the art of "doing well is the ultimate revenge".

A special note to my daughters, Ashley and Alexis. Although you have not been in my life physically, day in and day out, you have been there mentally and spiritually each and every day. This book was written so that you can be proud of Dad and hopefully learn something as well.

For all of my readers, if you are currently experiencing identity theft, have a friend or family member who has been or is being wrongfully sued because of identity theft, visit my website, at www.ediscoverynow.net or, visit my Internet Radio Show at www.blogtalkradio.com/ediscoverynutsandbolts, every for a live broadcast or podcast on identity theft protection and prevention.

ABOUT THE AUTHOR

Anthony Johnson is certified mediator, arbitration, negotiator, author, consultant, and E-Discovery House Counsel for eDiscovery Solutions, Inc. He has over 20 years' experience in an eclectic mix of consumer related issues including, consumer debt, medical debt, foreclosure, financial arbitration, wrongful termination, FDCPA, FCRA, and E-Discovery Project Management.

He earned a Diploma in Law from the University of London (U.K.), a bachelor's and master's degree in the liberal arts from Christian Bible College and Seminary. He also attended the prestigious Harvard Program on Negotiation, Adams State College, and Lakewood College, for mediation, arbitration and negotiation, an alumni of Bryan University's E-Discovery Project Management Graduate program, and is a candidate for an LL.M in International Business and Finance at the University of Liverpool (U.K.).

Anthony is a member of the American Bar Association, Juripax Online Dispute Resolution, and is the founder of the National Association for E-Discovery Professionals. He is also the Founder, President and CEO of eDiscovery Solutions, Inc., a company that specializes in E-Discovery Project Management Consultation.

Anthony has authored 12 ebooks on E-Discovery in his "eDiscovery Nuts and Bolts" series (three of which are digital textbooks for students throughout the country) and has authored 4 books in his series of nonfiction and fiction "crisis of the day" short stories on the current consumer debt crisis. His first book, "Too Big For Fraud" is his fictional debut international legal thriller about the mortgage foreclosure crisis. His second book entitled, "A Debtor's Burden" is about how consumers can successfully challenge consumer debt and restore their good name. His third book, "Medical Deficit Disorder" is about how patients can challenge medical debt, eliminate most if not all the debt, without filing bankruptcy, and restore their good name. And, "Too Big For Fraud (E-Discovery for Foreclosure)" is his non-fictional sequel to "Too Big For Fraud" the fictional "crisis of the day" short story.

All are available online or wherever books are sold.